# ISLAM

## by Dr. Harold J. Berry

Former Professor of Bible & Greek
Grace University
Omaha, Nebraska

BACK TO THE BIBLE
*Publishing*

ISLAM
published by Back to the Bible
©1992 by Harold J. Berry
All rights reserved.

*International Standard Book Number*
*0-8474-0831-0*

For information:
BACK TO THE BIBLE
POST OFFICE BOX 82808
LINCOLN, NEBRASKA 68501

6 7 8 9 10 11 12—04 03 02 01 00 99
Printed in the USA

# ISLAM

Every human being is born a Muslim, according to Muslims. They have this concept because they believe their God, Allah, is the only source of all life.

As children grow to maturity, it is thought by Muslims that they will accept Islam as their religion if they are allowed to have access to Islam and to develop their innate nature.[1]

The terms "Islam" and "Muslim" may be new to some, but they are becoming increasingly common in this world, where one out of every five people is a Muslim.

"Islam" is the name of the religion. Among other things, this word means "submission" or "peace," with peace being the Muslim concept of submission to Allah.

"Muslim" (sometimes spelled Moslem) refers to a follower of Islam. A Muslim is one who is submitted to Allah's will.

No ceremony is involved in becoming a Muslim. All one needs to do is say, "There is no god but God, and Muhammad is the Prophet of God." Once a person declares these two Islamic concepts—that God is the only God and that Muhammad is His Prophet—no more is required as proof of his faith. From that point forward, such a person has all the rights granted under Islamic law, and he is also obligated by all its duties.[2]

Islam is one of the fastest growing religions in the world. It has become the religion of the majority of people in many countries. Some report that Muslims constitute 85 percent of the population in 32 countries and between 25 and 85 percent in 11 other countries.[3]

It is impossible to establish with certainty how many Muslims live in the United States. Some estimate there are two to three million Muslims in the

United States.[4] Others say there are "four million or so."[5] Some predict that Muslims will become the second largest religious community in the U.S. in about ten years.[6]

There are now 11 million Muslims in Western Europe.[7] The growth of Islam has been phenomenal. According to Anis A. Shorrosh, Islamic mosques (places of worship) in France grew in number from only one in 1974 to 1500 in 1988.[8] Shorrosh is a Christian Arab who has written an insightful and helpful book defending the deity of Christ and the superiority of the Bible to the Quran (also spelled Koran).

Islamic mosques and centers seem to be everywhere in the United States. A check of your telephone directory will indicate if one exists in your area and where it is located. Some are elaborate and attention grabbing; others are plain and inconspicuous.

Islam is also advancing in the Soviet Union. *Christianity Today* reported that 120 mosques were opened in the northern Caucasus region of the

U.S.S.R. during 1990 and that another 50 were waiting to be registered. Although very few Soviet Muslims had been allowed to make the trip to Mecca in past years, 1500 were allowed to make the trip during 1990.[9]

What is the background of this fast-growing religion? Who or what is responsible for having taken a billion people worldwide into the fold of Islam?

## Background

The most prominent person in regard to Islam is Muhammad (sometimes spelled Mohammed). The Muslims are offended, however, if they are referred to as "Muhammadans." This gives the impression, they believe, that they worship Muhammad, whereas they emphasize that they worship none but Allah.

Muslims consider Islam to be a universal religion. They believe that it has always existed—even before Muhammad came on the scene. So they do not speak of his having founded Islam but only of his having restored it.[10]

Muhammad was born at Mecca (in what is now Saudi Arabia) in A.D. 570. His father, 'Abdu'llah, was a leading citizen of the area, but he died just before Muhammad was born. Muhammad was actually named by his grandfather, 'Abdu'l-Muttalib. On hearing of his son's death, he went to his daughter-in-law's house, took the baby in his arms and called him "Muhammad," which means "The Praised One."[11]

As was the custom of the Quraish tribe in those days 'Amina, Muhammad's mother, gave him to a woman in one of the Bedouin tribes so he could be nursed by her in the open air of the desert. This was thought to produce healthier children.

Reports differ on how long this arrangement lasted. But apparently this was done until he was about five years old, with the Bedouin nurse occasionally bringing him back to his mother.

When Muhammad was finally returned to his mother, she took him on a trip to Yathrib (later called Medina). But she died on the way back home. After his mother's death, Muhammad was cared for by his grandfather, who died two years later. Muhammad was then raised by his father's brother, Abu Talib.

Nothing seems to be unusual about Muhammad's boyhood and early youth. Occasionally he traveled with his uncle to Damascus and other cities.

He became proficient enough at the trading business in these caravans that at 25 he entered into the service of a rich widow, Khadijah, who lived in Mecca. She was so impressed with his service that she offered to marry him, even though she was 15 years older than he was. Muhammad accepted and was deeply devoted to her. As long as she lived, he took no other wife.

To Muhammad and Khadijah were born six children—four daughters and two sons. The sons both died in infancy. One of his daughters, Fatima, married Abu Talib's son, Ali. This couple would figure prominently in later Islamic endeavors to trace the line of authority from Muhammad.

After his wife's death, Muhammad took other wives. In all, he eventually had 15 wives, which is significant when the Quran (which later came from his revelations) allowed for only four wives. "From several historical accounts," says Shorrosh, "it is clear that he married someone new every year after Khadijah's death."[12] According to Shorrosh, 'Ayisha, the youngest of his eleven wives, "used to say that the prophet loved three things—women, scents, and food."[13] Muhammad had married 'Ayisha when she was only 10 years old.

Muslims explain these marriages (differing on the number of wives) as being partly for political reasons and partly out of pity for the wives whose husbands had been killed in battle defending the Islamic community.[14]

Some of the chroniclers of Muhammad's life point out that many things were troubling Muhammad. He had experienced some tragic circumstances early in his life, and the death of his sons had left him without an heir (by the standards of that day). In addition, other burdens were weighing him down. Throughout Mecca in the bazaars and shrines, the ancient virtues of honor and generosity seemed to be eroding.[15]

Muhammad was an introspective man. While living in Mecca he withdrew each year to a cave on Mount Hira in the nearby desert. There he meditated and prayed for several days. During the month of Ramadan (the ninth month of the Islamic calendar), as Muhammad was meditating in a cave, a voice called out to him, "Recite!" At first he was frightened. He did not understand what he was to recite. Then the voice said, "In the name of thy Lord the Creator, who created mankind from a clot of blood, recite!"[16]

Muhammad was extremely disturbed as he went home to his wife. He was afraid he was possessed by an evil spirit. Khadijah consoled him and then called for her cousin, an elderly convert to Christianity. He assured Muhammad that he was not crazy but that "he had experienced a true revelation like those God had allowed Moses and the prophets, and Muhammad must submit to it."[17]

The counsel this elderly man gave Muhammad significantly affected his understanding of God and religion. Just as other converts have not necessarily had a clear grasp of biblical Christianity, so this was true of Khadijah's cousin. He had been largely influenced by a Nestorian view of Christianity, especially concerning the person of Jesus Christ. The beliefs of Nestorius will be further delineated when considering the beliefs of the Muslims.

The revelations continued for Muhammad, and they were later recorded in what is called the Quran, which means "recite."

Muhammad never claimed that he was proclaiming a new religion. He believed that what had been revealed to him was the same religion revealed to other prophets, such as Abraham,

Moses, Solomon, Jonah and Jesus. Muhammad thought, however, that the religion revealed to the earlier prophets had become corrupted and that he was now restoring it to its original purity.

Muhammad emphasized monotheism, the belief in one God. This brought him into conflict with his fellow Meccans, who believed in polytheism (many gods). In particular, the cubed stone building known as the Ka'aba had 360 idols of the local Arab tribes. It also had a black stone "alleged to have been given to the first man, Adam, and subsequently found by the patriarch Abraham to identify the place of Allah's worship."[18]

Because the Arabs trace their lineage through Abraham's son Ishmael, they also associate Ishmael with the Ka'aba. It is believed that the Ka'aba "was first built by Abraham and his son Ishmael for worship of the one true God."[19]

The Muslims believe that it was Ishmael, not Isaac, who was to have been sacrificed by Abraham, although the Quran does not specify that. One of their reasons for believing this is that the son is referred to as an "only" son (Gen. 22:2). Isaac was not born until Ishmael was 14, so they reason that the "only" son had to be Ishmael. This disregards the fact that Hebrews 11:17 refers to Isaac as Abraham's "only be-gotten" son. The Greek word translated "only begotten" does not refer to birth but to a unique relationship. So even though Abraham had two sons, Isaac could be referred to as an "only" son in this distinct sense.

Muhammad's anti-idolatry message in Mecca made him an enemy of the city. Opposition to his views continued to escalate until finally, in 622, he was forced to flee to Medina (then known as Yathrib), about 250 miles north of Mecca. His flight was known as the "Hegira" (also spelled Hejira). The name of the city was later changed to Medina, which means "City of the Prophet."

Islam shifted at this point from a monotheistic *religion* to a monotheistic *philosophy* of religion, politics and daily life. Muhammad was offered leadership in Yathrib, and he took it.

So significant was Muhammad's flight from Mecca to Medina that the year (622) became the first year in the Islamic calendar. Dates are noted as A.H.—After Hegira.

At first, Muhammad apparently expected the Jews and Christians to accept him as a prophet. He even originally chose Jerusalem as the direction to be faced during prayer. But when the Jews of Medina aligned with his enemies in Mecca, Muhammad "drove them from the city and organized a purely Moslem society. To symbolize the independence of the new religion, he ordered Moslems to face Mecca, instead of Jerusalem, when praying."[20]

Muhammad gathered forces together that enabled him to conquer Mecca in 630. He destroyed the idols in the Ka'aba and proclaimed it a "mosque." Two years later Muhammad died, and his tomb is in the Prophet's Mosque in Medina.

Church historian Earle E. Cairns comments, "The greatest gains of this new dynamic faith took place between 632 and 732. Syria and Palestine were won by 640, and the Mosque of Omar was soon erected in Jerusalem."[21]

Although Muslims consider it a weakness of Christianity that there are so many different groups within it, there are also many sects within Islam—some say more than 150.[22] The largest sects in Islam are the Sunnis and the Shi'ites. About 90 percent of all Muslims are Sunnis, who trace their heritage to Muhammad's first four spiritual and political successors.

The Shi'ites are the next largest sect of Islam. The Shi'ites insist that the true line from Muhammad came through his son-in-law, Ali. (Muhammad's daughter Fatima had married Ali, the son of Abu Talib.).

Some of the other sects in Islam are the Sufis, Alawites, Takfirs and the Wahhabis.

# Beliefs

Although the background of a religious group may be interesting, that which matters most is their beliefs. If people are to be helped not only for time but also for eternity, it is essential that they believe the truth revealed by God concerning Himself and the salvation He offers.

Muslims adhere to what is commonly called "The Five Pillars." These Pillars are the recital of the creed, prayer, fasting, almsgiving and pilgrimage.

The creed is: "There is no god but God, and Muhammad is the Prophet of God." (The Arabic word for "God" is "Allah.") Some believe if this creed is recited—even if the person does not understand what he is saying—he becomes a Muslim. Others say it must be said in Arabic with intent and with the right index finger raised.

Muslims offer prayer five times a day while facing Mecca. Fasting is observed from sunrise to sunset during the month of Ramadan, the month when Gabriel supposedly delivered the Quran to Muhammad. Almsgiving is emphasized by the Muslims, who are to give to charity at least two and a half percent of their annual net income. A pilgrimage to Mecca is an obligation of every Muslim at least once in his lifetime if he is "mentally, financially and physically fit."[23]

These are The Five Pillars of Islam, but more detailed beliefs need to be compared with biblical Christianity.

Source of Authority

Of all the important questions to ask regarding a religious group, none is more important than inquiring about what it considers to be its final source of authority.

Islam holds to the Quran as its final authority. Muslims believe that the Quran was dictated to Muhammad by the angel Gabriel and that it was later recorded in Arabic.

The Quran is given the highest reverence by the Muslims. "They dare not touch it without first being washed and purified. They read it with the greatest care and respect, never holding it below their waist," says Shorrosh.[24]

The Quran is a little smaller in size than the Christian New Testament. It is divided into Surahs, or chapters, which grow progressively shorter from beginning to end. Those at the end are the first revelations Muhammad received, so chronological development is seen as one reads the Quran from the back to the front.

Muslims consider the Quran to be the perfect revelation from God. They believe it is a faithful reproduction of an original that was engraved on a tablet in heaven, which has existed from all eternity.[25]

Although the Quran was written 500-600 years after the New Testament was penned, "seventy-five percent of the glorious Quran . . . is from the Holy Bible," observes Shorrosh, an Arabic-speaking Christian.[26]

In contrast to the Bible, which has been freely copied and translated, the

18

Muslims maintain that the Quran cannot be adequately expressed in any other written form. "It is impossible," they say, "to reproduce the meaning, beauty, and fascination of the Qur'an in any other form."[27]

The Islamic Society of North America, however, is considering producing a more readable Quran. In particular, the Society is concerned about the need for a "more relevant Koran complete with commentary."[28]

In addition to the Quran, the Muslims also hold to traditions about Muhammad. They believe he was directed by God in all that he said and did, so Muslims depend on these traditions to guide them in every area of life—personal, social and political, as well as religious.

The Muslim method of handling the Christian Scriptures is seen in what they say about Ishmael, who they believe was to have been the offering instead of Isaac, as mentioned previously. They quote Genesis 22:2, which refers to an "only" son, but they totally disregard the rest of the passage that refers to Isaac. Such an arbitrary selection of some biblical data and the rejection of others shows that their interpretation is decided by presuppositions.

As to source of authority, biblical Christianity accepts only the 66 books of the Bible. The original manuscripts were written over a period of 1600 years by at least 40 authors whom God inspired to write exactly as He willed. Moses was inspired to write the Pentateuch (first five books) about 1500 B.C., and the Apostle John was inspired to write his epistles and Revelation near the end of the first century, A.D.

Biblical Christianity considers the original manuscripts to be the written Word of God recorded without error (see Matt. 5:18; II Tim. 3:16; II Pet. 1:21). The 39 books of the Old Testament were written in Hebrew (with small portions in Aramaic), and the 27 books of the New Testament were written in Greek.

Inspiration is not claimed for copies or translations of these original manuscripts. Although the original manuscripts are no longer available, a sufficient number of early copies have been found to reconstruct the originals. No one needs to doubt that what is available in various translations is essentially what was in the original manuscripts.

Trinity

Muslims are repelled by the thought of a Trinity (that God is a tri-unity). They consider such a belief to be polytheism—the belief in many gods. Muslims, as do the Jews, believe God is an absolute rather than a composite unity. Perhaps this is why Muhammad at first did not expect opposition from the Jews. Most probably, however, Muhammad's views of Christianity first came from those who denied the Trinity.

Some think that the Muslim concept of Allah and the Christian concept of Jehovah are the same God referred to by different names. But some who are knowledgeable of both religions strongly disagree. S. M. Zwemer, missionary to the Muslims in a past generation, raised the question, "Is the statement of the Koran true, 'Your God and our God is the same'?"[29] He answered his own question when he said, "In as far as Moslems are monotheists and in as far as Allah has many of the attributes of Jehovah we cannot put Him with the false gods. But neither can there be any doubt that Mohammed's conception of God is inadequate, incomplete, barren and grievously distorted."[30]

In particular, Zwemer pointed out that Islam's concept of God has no emphasis on His Fatherhood. Also, their God is seriously lacking in the attribute of love, and He is not "absolutely, unchangeably and eternally just." He also noted that the attributes of the Muslim Allah lack harmony.[31]

Muslims never refer to Allah as "Father." To do so, they reason, would be to imply they are His children, or even equal with God. For this reason they also avoid expressions such as "sons of God" and "children of God." God would need a wife, they reason, in order for Him to have children. Rather than viewing themselves in a father-son relationship, Muslims view their relationship with God as a master-slave relationship.

Biblical Christianity accepts the teaching that God is a Trinity. The three Persons of the Godhead are one, though distinct. The Father, Son and Holy Spirit comprise a composite unity. G. W. Bromiley, writing in *Evangelical Dictionary of Theology*, says, "Within the one essence of the Godhead we have to distinguish three 'persons' who are neither three gods on the one side, nor three parts or modes of God on the other, but coequally and coeternally God."[32]

In the Old Testament, the plural pronouns used for God indicate the three Persons of the one Godhead (see Gen. 1:26; 11:7). A careful examination of the Christian Scriptures reveals that each of the three Persons of the one Godhead possesses divine attributes. Each is omnipresent, omnipotent, omniscient; and each receives worship, which only God is allowed to do.

The distinctiveness of the three Persons in the one Godhead is seen from Matthew 28:19 where "name" is singular, although the three Persons—Father, Son and Holy Spirit—are mentioned.

Trinitarian statements about the Godhead are found in the Apostles' Creed—one of the oldest creeds in existence. It was known to be used as early as A.D. 150, more than 400 years before Muhammad was born.[33]

Jesus Christ

In contrasting the beliefs of Islam and biblical Christianity, a special concern is what each believes about the deity, atonement and prophethood of the Lord Jesus Christ.

*His Deity*

Islam denies the deity of Christ. Muslims teach that Jesus Christ never claimed to be God or referred to Himself as the Son of God.[34] They are especially repelled by the thought of Jesus Christ's being referred to as the "Son of God." To them, this implies that God has a wife in order for a child to be born. This is understandably a blasphemous thought to them.

Biblical Christianity teaches that Jesus Christ is God—that He is the second Person of the Trinity. John 1:1 states, "In the beginning was the Word, and the Word was with God, and the Word was God." Verse 14 makes clear who is referred to as the "Word": "The Word was made flesh, and dwelt among us." Only Jesus Christ fits the qualifications of the one referred to.

Although He has existed from eternity past, the Lord Jesus Christ took upon Himself human form so that He could give His life on the cross for the sin of the world. When He came into the world, the Heavenly Father declared, "Let all the angels of God worship him" (Heb. 1:6). The fact that

25

worship is ascribed to Jesus Christ is an indication that He is God, for Jesus Himself later told Satan, "Thou shalt worship the Lord thy God, and him only shalt thou serve" (Matt. 4:10).

Biblical Christianity makes no claim that God "begat" Jesus in the physical sense of the word. That would be considered blasphemous to Christians as well. As God, the Lord Jesus Christ has always existed. But in the miracle of the Incarnation, He took on Himself human form as He was born to Mary, who conceived by means of the Holy Spirit (see Luke 1:26-35).

The angel Gabriel told Mary, "The Holy Spirit will come upon you, and the power of the Most High will over-shadow you; and for that reason the holy offspring shall be called the Son of God" (v. 35, NASB).

Although the word "son" in Scripture is often used to mean "descendant," it does not always mean that. According to the flesh, Jesus was a descendant of

David because He was born in the line of Judah.

As indicated in John 5:18, however, there is another sense in which the Father-Son relationship applied to Jesus. The Jews wanted to kill Jesus because He not only was healing on the Sabbath, but He was also calling God "his Father." How did the Jews understand Jesus' statement? (Calling God His Father was the same as saying He was the Son of God.) The Jews clearly understood that such a claim had nothing to do with being a descendant of God. They understood that He was "making himself equal with God." This is why they wanted to kill Him. Had He not claimed to be equal with God, they would not have been so incensed. They highly revered Abraham, Moses and the prophets. Had Jesus claimed to be a prophet or someone highly regarded but less than God, it is unlikely the Jews would have sought to kill Him.

If Jesus Christ were only God, He could not have died on the cross for the sin of the world. If He were only man,

His death could not have paid the penalty for the sins of others. It was necessary for Him to be the God-Man.

Throughout the centuries of church history, not all have agreed that Jesus Christ is the God-Man. Nestorius, patriarch of Constantinople for three years (428-431), was such a person. He became the founder of the Nestorian Church, which had many followers in Persia (present-day Iran). Nestorius denied the biblical teaching that Jesus Christ was the God-Man come to earth to redeem fallen mankind. To Nestorius, "Christ was in effect only a perfect man who was morally linked to deity."[35]

Nestorius's views were condemned in 431 at the Council of Nicea at Ephesus, 139 years before Muhammad was born. It was believed then—and should be remembered now—that if Jesus Christ were less than God, He would not have been able to save mankind. The views of Nestorius were not considered an orthodox view of Christianity from that time onward.

Muhammad's early contact with Christianity likely came from those who held the views of Nestorius about Jesus Christ—that He was only a man and not God. This would have significantly influenced Muhammad regarding what he thought biblical Christianity taught.

*His Atonement*

Islam denies the death of Jesus Christ on the cross to pay for the penalty of sin. Muslims believe that He was taken to heaven by God before having to go to the cross. They believe that whoever died on the cross was only someone who appeared to be like Jesus but that it was not He.

Hammudah Abdalati, a Muslim, says, "Islam rejects the doctrine of the Crucifixion of Jesus by the enemies of God and also the foundations of the doctrine. This rejection is based on the authority of God Himself as revealed in the Qur'an, and on a deeper rejection of blood sacrifice and vicarious atonement for sins."[36] This is an interesting statement inasmuch as a lamb is sacrificed in many Muslim homes on the feast day every year.

Because the blood of bulls and goats could not take away sin, the Lord Jesus Christ took upon Himself a human body so that He could shed His blood for the sins of the world (see Heb. 10:4,5).

The Bible says, "Almost all things are by the law purged with blood; and without shedding of blood is no remission [forgiveness]" (Heb. 9:22). The Scriptures also reveal that "the blood of Jesus Christ . . . cleanseth us from all sin" (I John 1:7).

*His Prophethood*

Muslims see no difference between Jesus Christ and Muhammad, other than saying that Muhammad is the last (and the seal) of all the prophets. The Quran states, "Say (O Muslims): We believe in Allah and that which is revealed unto us and that which was revealed unto Abraham, and Ishmael, and Isaac, and Jacob, and the tribes, and that which Moses and Jesus received, and that which the Prophets received from their Lord. We make no distinctions between any of them, and unto Him we have surrendered" (2:136).[37]

How can the Muslims make no distinctions between Jesus Christ and Muhammad? The only way they can put Muhammad on the same level with Jesus Christ is to discredit the eyewitness reports of the New Testament concerning Christ.

No one could legitimately accuse Jesus Christ of any weakness, let alone any sin. The disciples, who were with Him constantly, never accused him of a single fault. Jesus once asked an audience, "Which one of you convicts Me of sin? If I speak truth, why do you not believe Me?" (John 8:46, NASB). The testimony of the apostles was emphatically expressed by Peter, who said that Jesus never committed a sin nor was He ever deceitful (I Pet. 2:22).

The reason such a testimony could be given concerning Jesus was that

31

there was no sin in Him (Heb. 4:15; I Pet. 1:19; I John 3:5). No such claims were made for Muhammad by his close companions as were made for the Lord Jesus Christ by the apostles in their eyewitness New Testament reports.

Admittedly, it is one thing to claim to be sinless and to be God; it is quite another to prove those claims. The resurrection of Jesus Christ from the dead proved that His claims were true. In Paul's great sermon on Mars Hill, he proclaimed that God will someday judge the world through Jesus Christ. To confirm his statement, Paul added, "Having furnished proof to all men by raising Him from the dead" (Acts 17:31, NASB).

First Corinthians 15 is commonly called "The Resurrection Chapter" of the Bible. The Apostle Paul recorded that after Jesus Christ's resurrection, He "was seen of Cephas [Peter], then of the twelve: After that, he was seen of above five hundred brethren at once; of whom the greater part remain unto this present, but some are fallen asleep" (vv. 5,6).

In effect, Paul was saying, "Even though some of this group have died, most are still living. If you don't believe what I'm saying about Christ's resurrection, go ask them."

Although Jesus' tomb is empty—as verified by believers and unbelievers—Muhammad's remains are in the Prophet's Mosque in Medina. There is no valid comparison between Jesus Christ and Muhammad.

## Holy Spirit

The Quran makes few references to the Holy Spirit. "Muslim theologians are at a loss to explain what is meant by the Holy Spirit," says Shorrosh.[38] In spite of what Muslims believe, Shorrosh accurately emphasizes, "Never once does the Holy Spirit in any text of the Bible refer to Muhammad, the Quran, or Islam."[39] The Scriptures reveal that the Holy Spirit is a person because He does things only a person can do. He convicts, guides, discloses things to come and glorifies Christ (see John

16:7-15). He searches the depths of God and knows the thoughts of God (see I Cor. 2:10,11). It is also possible for the Holy Spirit to be grieved (see Eph. 4:30).

The Bible also teaches that the Holy Spirit is God. In Acts 5:3,4 He is called God. The Holy Spirit does what only God can do—He regenerates by giving new birth to those who trust in Jesus Christ for salvation (see John 3:3-8).

## Man/Woman

Of all the contrasts between Islam and Christianity, one of the most apparent is the different attitudes of men toward women. The Quran says, "Men are in charge of women, because Allah hath made the one of them to excel the other, and because they spend of their property (for the support of women). So good women are the obedient, guarding in secret that which Allah hath guarded. As for those from whom ye fear rebellion, admonish them and banish them to beds apart, and scourge them" (4:34).

Muslim writers make it seem that Islam has only positive benefits to womanhood, but those who are close observers do not share the same opinion.

Having seen the practical outworkings of Islam, Shorrosh says, "A Muslim husband may cast his wife adrift without giving a single reason or even notice. The husband possesses absolute, immediate, and unquestioned power of divorce. No privilege of a corresponding nature is reserved for the wife."[40] Although some people debate how easy it is for a Muslim husband to divorce his wife, all agree that a Muslim wife does not have equal rights.

The Bible sets forth the equality of woman and man. They are considered "one in Christ" (Gal. 3:28), which gives equal standing before Him.

Christian husbands are commanded: "Love your wives, even as Christ also loved the church, and gave himself for it" (Eph. 5:25). The word translated "love" refers to an act of the will whereby the husband is to seek the highest good of his wife.

Muslims may claim that their men are seeking the highest good of the four wives and unlimited number of concubines (sexual partners) the Quran allows them, but others would seriously question this. The Bible nowhere indicates God's approval of sexual relationships between unmarried persons; instead, it commands believers to flee adultery and fornication.

## Sin

Islam believes that man is born into the world in a pure state and that what he becomes depends on external circumstances.[41]

In responding to David Shenk's views of Christianity's concept of sin and evil, Badru Kateregga says, "Muslims believe that man is fundamentally a good and dignified creature. He is not a fallen being. Muslims certainly would not agree that even prophets have participated in sinfulness!"[42]

Such views caused Zwemer to say, "Islam denies the doctrine of the atonement and minimizes the heinousness of sin." [43] Apart from the Lord Jesus Christ, all have sinned and come short of the glory of God (Rom. 3:23).

Biblical Christianity and Islam differ significantly on the concept of sin. The Bible teaches that when Adam and Eve faced a choice in the Garden of Eden, they chose to go their own way instead of God's way (see Gen. 3). Because of this sin by the head of the human race (Adam), a sinful nature has been passed down to all descendants.

David acknowledged that he was brought forth in iniquity and that his mother had conceived him in sin (see Ps. 51:5). He was not referring to any immoral act of his mother but to the sinful condition of mankind as they enter the world.

Romans 5:12 reveals that sin came into the world through one man (Adam) and that as a result, death passed to all men. Proof of this is that all will eventually die. Romans 6:23 emphasizes that death is the result of sin. Muhammad's tomb in the Prophet's Mosque in Medina proves he is no exception.

Salvation

Salvation in Islam is based on a works righteousness. Each Muslim is viewed as having his deeds weighed on a giant scale. If the good deeds outweigh the bad, he is allowed to enter paradise.

"In Islam, it is believed that God judges people by their deeds or works, not by rites or ceremonies such as baptism. Islam further denies that a human can attain religious felicity on the basis of faith alone," says Faruqi.[44]

Because salvation in Islam is always a goal in this life, not an attainment, Faruqi observes, "Religious justification is . . . the Muslims' eternal hope, never their complacent certainty, not for even a fleeting moment."[45]

The Bible reveals that because mankind is sinful, the only hope is to trust in the redemptive work of the Lord Jesus Christ. Any good works done by an individual are to no avail if the purpose is to obtain salvation on the basis of merit. The Old Testament Law system was based on works, but it was never intended to save anyone. The Book of Romans indicates that no one will be saved by the works of the Law. Salvation is possible only through the righteousness that comes by faith in Jesus Christ (see 3:19-23).

Before trusting in Jesus Christ for salvation, mankind is viewed as dead in trespasses and sins (Eph. 2:1). To those hoping to be saved by good works, Ephesians 2:8,9 says, "By grace are ye saved through faith; and that not of yourselves: it is the gift of God: not of works, lest any man should boast."

Good works are important—not as a means of salvation but as an evidence of it. Ephesians 2:10 states, "For we are his workmanship, created in Christ

Jesus unto good works, which God hath before ordained that we should walk in them." Good works are meaningless to God until a person acknowledges his sinful condition and trusts Christ as Saviour.

Islam rejects what the Bible says about sin and salvation. Kateregga, a Muslim, says, "Islam does not identify with the Christian conviction that man needs to be redeemed. The Christian belief in the redemptive sacrificial death of Christ does not fit the Islamic view that man has always been fundamentally good, and that God loves and forgives those who obey His will."[46]

In spite of such statements about man's being fundamentally good, the Muslims do see a need for special consideration by Allah. This is evident from their teaching concerning *Jihad*, or holy war. According to the Quran, those who die during a holy war are considered martyrs and earn immediate entrance into paradise (3:156-158).

The Quran also says, "And what though ye be slain in Allah's way or die therein? Surely pardon from Allah and mercy are better than all that they amass. What though ye be slain or die, when unto Allah ye are gathered?" (3:157,158).

George Grant, an observer of the Middle East Crisis and of Islamic advancement around the world, says, "Because *Ji'had* is an innate aspect of Islam, the ambition to conquer the world and subjugate the infidels has never been abandoned by the Moslems."[47] Grant believes that his point is proved by the "recent spate of terrorism—highjackings, bombings, kidnappings, attacks, and even direct military confrontation."[48]

Jihad, with its concept of immediate entrance into paradise because of being a martyr in a holy war, reveals a religious system based on human merit.

But all systems of human merit fail. Some people may merit more than others, but none can merit right standing before a holy God. This is why Titus 3:5 says, "Not by works of righteousness which we have done, but according to his mercy he saved us."

Future Life

One Muslim writer describes the route to one's eternal destiny this way: "When the trial is over those destined to Hell or Paradise will be made to pass over a narrow bridge to their respective destinations. The bridge is so fashioned that the favored will cross with ease and facility while the condemned will tumble off into Hell."[49]

Norman Anderson, editor of *The World's Religions* and author of the section on Islam, describes the Muslim concept of paradise. After the judging of their deeds, Anderson says, "Some will be admitted to paradise, where they will recline on soft couches quaffing cups of wine handed to them by the Huris, or maidens of paradise, of whom each man may marry as many as he pleases. Others will be consigned to the torments of hell. Almost all, it would seem, will have to enter the fire temporarily, but no true Muslim will remain there for ever."[50] As mentioned previously, martyrs in a holy war are guaranteed immediate access into paradise.

Biblical Christianity teaches that "it is appointed unto men once to die, but after this the judgment" (Heb. 9:27). Those who have trusted in Jesus Christ for salvation will be rewarded for their good deeds at the Judgment Seat of Christ (see I Cor. 3:11-15; II Cor. 5:10). This judgment, or evaluation, is not to determine salvation but rewards. Those who have rejected Christ as Saviour will be given the sentence of judgment at the Great White Throne Judgment (see Rev. 20:11-15).

Biblical Christianity offers the good news that those who trust Christ as Saviour in this life can be assured of their salvation and future destiny. The Apostle John wrote his first epistle so believers could know for certain that they had eternal life (I John 5:13). You do not need to wait until some final judgment to be sure of your salvation.

# Conclusion

Islam is more than a religion—it is a monotheistic philosophy of religion, politics and daily life. One Muslim explains that the Islamic state is not actually a state but a world order with a government, a court, a constitution and an army. He also indicates that to enter this Islamic state is to make a decision for peace with one's fellow humans in the community of Islam.[51]

Many thinkers would question this statement after seeing the terrorizing and brutalizing of Kuwait by their Muslim brothers in Iraq. And that followed on the heels of the Iran-Iraq eight-year war that pitted Muslim against Muslim and cost more than a million lives. Sometimes little peace is found in Islam, even though its followers emphasize that the name means "peace."

Christians are concerned, however, about more than acquiring peace in this life; it is also needed for eternity. So the question that needs to be answered is,

How does a person gain peace with God?

This kind of peace comes through a right standing with God by trusting Jesus Christ as Saviour. Through this decision a person is delivered from condemnation, and he acquires peace with God. The Bible tells us, "Being justified by faith, we have peace with God through our Lord Jesus Christ" (Rom. 5:1).

Any religion that makes the atoning work of Christ unnecessary and places emphasis on human merit cannot provide eternal salvation or peace with God.

But here is the crux of the matter: Does a person believe that the *Bible* contains the written Word of God or that the *Quran* contains it—or both? If the Bible is accepted as the source of authority, no choice is left but to reject all systems that deny the deity of Jesus Christ and His atoning work on the cross.

How, then, are we to reach Muslims with the Gospel of the death, burial and resurrection of the Lord Jesus Christ?

Those who have worked in Muslim ministries for years affirm that it is not an easy task. They do give us some guidelines, however.

One person actively involved in a ministry to Muslims says, "Urge the Muslim friend to take the Gospel and compare the teachings of the Gospel to that of their Koran. Tell them to compare the Christ of the Gospel to the Christ of the Koran. Never be afraid that the Christ of the Gospel will come up second best—He never will. There have been many conversions to Christ by using this very method."

Another suggests, "If we do not believe that God is able to save Muslims of course there is no sense in our trying to win them. But if we believe that He intended that they should be included in the outreach of the church we must certainly believe that He is able to effect their salvation. This is the absolutely essential foundation to any effective witness to Muslims."[52]

The Lord may be using world circumstances to crack the Islamic veil.

Raymond Buker, Jr., for 15 years a missionary to the Muslims in Pakistan, says the defeat of Muslim military powers in the past has caused Muslims to question their beliefs. He adds, "The Iraqi defeat during the recent 'Operation Desert Storm' may well cause a similar questioning in the minds of Muslims. This disillusionment could open many to the gospel, even as conflict has opened Iran to the gospel in spite of persecution. The church there has tripled. In this country and in Muslim countries, thinking people are open to the gospel, and are turning to God."[53]

Those who work with Muslims also emphasize that, above all else, love for the people must be genuine. Even though Muslims disagree with our message, we must not be unkind. As Christians, we should evidence the fruit of the Spirit, as expressed in Galatians 5:22,23. We Christians must practice what we preach if we expect to receive a hearing from those who are seeking a relationship with God. Our lives must not make a lie out of what we believe.

Also, we must never depart from emphasizing the truth of the Scriptures. Although Muslims may reject that message, we are not helpful to them nor faithful to ourselves or to the Lord if we stop proclaiming the truth of the Scriptures.

Only the Scriptures are able to make a person wise unto salvation. And that salvation is available only through faith in the Lord Jesus Christ (see II Tim. 3:15). There is no hope in any other plan of salvation. "Neither is there salvation in any other: for there is none other name under heaven given among men, whereby we must be saved" (Acts 4:12).

The key to our message must be the death, burial and resurrection of the Lord Jesus Christ, which were confirmed by eyewitnesses (I Cor. 15:1-8). This is the Gospel, or good news, that we must proclaim to lost mankind, regardless of their religious affiliation. Regrettably, this is the very message that Muslims and the Quran deny.

But let us take hope. Many also doubted the resurrection of Christ in

Paul's day, but he kept on "preaching Jesus and the resurrection" (Acts 17:18, NASB). We must do the same. It is the resurrection of Christ that makes Christianity distinctly different from—and far superior to—other world religions.

But information and logic alone will not open closed hearts—only prayer is able to do that. It is significant that when Paul was preaching in Philippi, Luke recorded concerning Lydia that the "Lord opened her heart to respond to the things spoken by Paul" (16:14, NASB).

Let us keep proclaiming the Gospel of Christ, while at the same time praying and depending on the Lord to open hearts.

# Notes

[1]Hammudah, Abdalati. *Islam in Focus* (Indianapolis, IN: American Trust Publications, 1975), p. 16.

[2]Isma'il R. Al Faruqi, *Islam* (Niles, IL: Argus Communications, 1979), p. 4.

[3]Daniel Pipes, "The Muslims Are Coming! The Muslims Are Coming!" in *National Review*, November 19, 1990, p. 30.

[4]*Ibid.*, p. 31.

[5]*The Los Angeles Times*, cited in the *Omaha World-Herald*, April 6, 1991, p. 56.

[6]Pipes, "The Muslims Are Coming! The Muslims Are Coming!" in *National Review*, November 19, 1990, p. 31.

[7]*Ibid.*

[8]Anis A. Shorrosh, *Islam Revealed: A Christian Arab's View of Islam*

(Nashville, TN: Thomas Nelson Publishers, 1988), p. 172.

[9]*Christianity Today*, November 19, 1990, p. 60.

[10]Abdalati, *Islam in Focus*, p. 8.

[11]Shorrosh, *Islam Revealed*, p. 48.

[12]*Ibid.*, p. 56.

[13]*Ibid.*, p. 50.

[14]Caesar E. Farah, *Islam: Beliefs and Observances* (Woodbury, NY: Barron's Educational Series, Inc., 1968), p. 68.

[15]*The March of Islam: TimeFrame AD 600-800* (Richmond, VA: Time-Life Books, Inc., 1988), p. 32.

[16]*Ibid.*, p. 33.

[17]*Ibid.*

[18]Shorrosh, *Islam Revealed*, p. 51.

[19]Faruqi, *Islam*, p. 81.

[20]Charles J. Adams, "Mohammed," in *The World Book Encyclopedia*, Vol.13 (Chicago, IL: Field Enterprises Educational Corporation, 1973), p. 574.

[21]Earle E. Cairns, *Christianity Through the Centuries: A History of the Christian Church* (Grand Rapids, MI: Zondervan Publishing House, 1954, 1981), p. 173.

[22]Shorrosh, *Islam Revealed*, p. 281.

[23]Abdalati, *Islam in Focus*, p. 99.

[24]Shorrosh, *Islam Revealed*, p. 21.

[25]*Eerdmans' Handbook to the World's Religions* (Grand Rapids, MI: Wm. B. Eerdmans Publishing Company, 1982), p. 315.

[26]Shorrosh, *Islam Revealed*, p. 271.

[27]Abdalati, *Islam in Focus*, p. 3.

[28]*The Los Angeles Times*, cited in the *Omaha World-Herald*, April 6, 1991, p. 56.

[29]S. M. Zwemer, *The Moslem Doctrine of God* (New York: American Tract Society, 1905), p. 107.

[30]*Ibid.*

[31]*Ibid.*, see pp. 109-116.

[32]G. W. Bromiley, "Trinity," in *Evangelical Dictionary of Theology*, Walter A. Elwell, ed. (Grand Rapids, MI: Baker Book House, 1984), p. 1112.

[33]Fulton J. Sheen and Mervin Monroe Deems, "Apostles' Creed," in *The World Book Encyclopedia*, Vol. 1 (Chicago: World Book, Inc., 1986), p. 530.

[34]Abdalati, *Islam in Focus*, p. 158.

[35]Cairns, *Christianity Through the Centuries*, p. 136.

[36]Abdalati, *Islam in Focus,* p. 159.

[37]All quotations from the Quran are taken from *The Meaning of the Glorious Koran: An Explanatory Translation by Mohammed Marmaduke Pickthall* (New York: New American Library, n.d.).

[38]Shorrosh, *Islam Revealed*, p. 219.

[39]*Ibid.*, p. 221.

[40]*Ibid.*, p. 167.

[41]Abdalati, *Islam in Focus*, p. 32.

[42]Badru D. Kateregga and David W. Shenk, *Islam and Christianity* (Ibadan, Nigeria: Daystar Press, 1980), p. 108.

[43]Zwemer, *The Moslem Doctrine of God*, p. 112.

[44]Faruqi, *Islam*, p. 5.

[45]*Ibid.*

[46]Kateregga and Shenk, *Islam and Christianity*, p. 141.

[47]George Grant, *The Blood of the Moon: The Roots of the Middle East Crisis* (Brentwood, TN: Woglemuth & Hyatt, Publishers, Inc., 1991), p. 69.

[48]*Ibid.*, p. 73.

[49]Farah, *Islam: Beliefs and Observances*, pp. 115,116.

[50]Norman Anderson, ed., *The World's Religions*, 4th ed.; (Grand Rapids, MI: Eerdmans Publishing Company, 1975), p. 117.

[51]Farah, *Islam: Beliefs and Observances*, p. 65.

[52]Francis R. Steele, *Islam: An Analysis* (Upper Darby, PA: Arab World Ministries, n.d.), p. 5.

[53]Raymond Buker, Jr., "Taking the Gospel to Abraham's Other Son," *IMPACT*, May 1991, p. 8.

## Summary

| | |
|---|---|
| **Name of Religion:** | Islam |
| **Name of Followers:** | Muslims |
| **Name of Founder:** | Muhammad (570-632) |
| **Most Holy City:** | Mecca |
| **Number of Followers:** | U.S.: About 3-4 million |
| | Worldwide: About 1 billion |

**Beliefs**

**Source of Authority**

## Trinity

# Jesus Christ

## Holy Spirit

## Man/Woman

Quran says, "Men are in charge of women, because Allah hath made the one of them to excel the other" ...............34

It is relatively easy for a Muslim husband to divorce his wife; wives are never granted the same right ...............35

## Sin

Believe that man is born into the world in a pure state; what he becomes depends on circumstances ...............36

Believe that man is fundamentally good and not a fallen being.......36

## Salvation

## Future Life

Some believe that eternal destinies will be decided after a trial.
People will cross over a bridge that is constructed in such

61

# Recommended Reading

Anderson, Norman, ed. *The World's Religions*. 4th ed. Grand Rapids, MI: Eerdmans Publishing Company, 1975.

*Eerdmans' Handbook to the World's Religions*. Grand Rapids, MI: Wm. B. Eerdmans Publishing Company, 1982.

Grant, George. *The Blood of the Moon: The Roots of the Middle East Crisis*. Brentwood, TN: Wolgemuth & Hyatt, Publishers, Inc., 1991.

McDowell, Josh, and Stewart, Don. *Handbook of Today's Religions*. San Bernardino, CA: Here's Life Publishers, Inc., 1983.

Shorrosh, Anis A. *Islam Revealed: A Christian Arab's View of Islam*. Nashville, TN: Thomas Nelson Publishers, 1988.

Back to the Bible is a nonprofit ministry dedicated to Bible teaching, evangelism and edification of Christians worldwide.

If we may assist you in knowing more about Christ and the Christian life, please write to us without obligation:

Back to the Bible
P.O. Box 82808
Lincoln, NE 68501